I have a word of love

word of love

LOIS
WYSE

for you

American Greetings Corporation
Cleveland, Ohio 44144

Published by American Greetings, American Road, Cleveland, Ohio 4414
First printing, June, 1971. Copyright, 1971, by Lois Wyse.
Library of Congress Catalogue Card Number: 75-157558
Printed in the United States of America
An American Greetings Book

Gratefully,
That's the word.

You

Though you give me all your worldly goods
They mean nothing without you
To share them.
Take care of you today.

Timeless

How do I know it is morning?
You are in my mind.
How do I know it is night?
You are in my heart.

Giving

You don't have to give me gifts
To prove your love,
And that's why I like it
When you do.

Cooking

Dust.
Clean.
Sweep.
There is no love in those.
But cooking?
Aah, that is love, my love.

Talking

I want to tell you everything.
I who am usually
Close-mouthed, reticent,
Private, unspeaking.
With you I loose the ties
And talk.

Is that one phase of love?

Communicating

I understand your touch
Better than your words.

Deceiving

Sometimes I must deceive me,
The better to love you.

Doubting

I know I love you
Because with you
I voice my doubts.

Listen

Love becomes a habit
The moment we no longer think about it.
So listen, darling.
I don't want to be a habit.

Tick Tick

Stop trying so hard
To learn what makes me tick.
Why don't you concentrate instead
On the things that stop my ticking?

Pride

I am proud of you.
Maybe that is why
Our love works.
For us.
And me.

Triumph

The most personal triumph
Is love.

A special dedication . . . Thanks again, Rob

The Author

Lois Wyse is the author of best-selling books of
love poetry, including "Love Poems For The Very Married",
"Are You Sure You Love Me?", and "I Love You Better Now",
as well as the popular non-fiction book, "Mrs. Success".
Her articles and poems appear regularly in numerous
magazines in the United States and abroad.

Lois Wyse, her husband Marc, and their two children,
Katherine and Robert, live in Shaker Heights, Ohio.